DANZAS CUBANAS

SUITE for PIANO SOLO
by ERNESTO LECUONA

—o—

CONTENTS

EDWARD B. MARKS MUSIC COMPANY / Exclusively Distributed By HAL•LEONARD CORPORATION

7777 W. BLUEMOUND RD. P.O. BOX 13819 MILWAUKEE, WI 53213

A Graciela Tariche de Gispert

NO HABLES MÁS!!
(SPEAK NO MORE)
DANZA

ERNESTO LECUONA

Allegro moderato

A Lizzie Morales De Batet

NO PUEDO CONTIGO
(I CANNOT MAKE YOU UNDERSTAND)
DANZA

ERNESTO LECUONA

A Armando Palacios, Gran Artista

AHÍ VIENE EL CHINO
(HERE COMES THE CHINAMAN)
DANZA

ERNESTO LECUONA

Allegro ma non troppo

Al Dr. Gonzalo Arostegui

POR QUÉ TE VAS?
(WHY DO YOU GO)
DANZA

ERNESTO LECUONA

Moderato

A Margot Rojas

LOLA ESTÁ DE FIESTA
(LOLA IS CELEBRATING)
DANZA

ERNESTO LECUONA

Poco più mosso

A Matilde Gonzalez Redin De Molina

EN TRES POR CUATRO
(IN THREE QUARTER TIME)
DANZA

ERNESTO LECUONA